1

Pariah's Manifesto: Prequel To Grandsons of the Revolution

By Al R Suarez

Table of Contents

Intro-

Taking advantage of a lull in my studies, as the semester has ended for now, am going to attempt to start my fifth book. Originally my book was going to be called "Grandsons of the Revolution" but this will work as a prequel to that. The grandsons are going to be the grandsons of Leon Trotsky, Malcolm X and Che Guevara who all have a connection to Mexico and were or are rebels in their own way like their grandfathers. Also like their grandfathers they have been turned into pariahs. Canek Sanchez Guevara was said to be "under CIA manipulation" for his stances against Fidel, but if you see Che in his last years he was distancing himself from Fidel based on ideological differences. Canek passed away in early 2015 in Mexico City at age 40, outliving his grandfather by a year, he was a world traveler and writer.

Malcom X's grandson, Malcolm Shabazz was falsely accused of burning his grandmother to death. He was called a common criminal, as his grandfather as well went through the criminal "justice" system at a young age. Shabazz the grandson was killed in Mexico City in 2013 while on a tour there. One of his goals was recently accomplished, for Mexico to recognize the black minority in the country.

Also Trotsky probably was defamed the most out of the three, by Nazis, Capitalists and Stalinists alike, his grandson Esteban, was even wounded in one of the attempts on Leon's life as a child in Mexico. Esteban has been accused of not being an Orthodox Trotskyist or "Trotskyist" enough, among other things, as he takes care of the Trotsky home converted into a museum where Trotsky's remains are buried in a suburb of Mexico City. But let us get back to the task at hand.

Pariah's Manifesto was an idea that occurred to me as a good title quite recently as there was a renewal of defamation against me by "activists". It does not just symbolize me but how activists have been defamed in general recently, and how they are dehumanized by the corporate media, such as BLM protesters (Black Lives Matter). I have been defamed so much over the years and the demons continue to come, that I am now embracing the pariah label and as a good activist using a disadvantage and making it an advantage in my manifesto, which continues with the same message of justice and revolution. May we inherit revolutionary spirit as was embodied in the original Occupy and other groups and movements, to make a better future for our children, may unity and solidarity come at last...

Tampa, Fl

Al R Suarez

12/13/15

Chapter I

Personality's Role In Revolution

The revolution is above differences of personality, and as warned in previous books, we must prevent a Napoleon or Stalin taking over the revolution. Being a comrade and a friend are two different things. Put your egos and differences aside for the cause as comrades, that is a revolutionary thing. The false prophet takes advantage of differences, instead of similarities. The provocateur is a divider not a uniter. Therefore, the cult of personality instigated by these false prophets, must be prevented. Which is not to say an organized leadership with charisma like that of Hugo Chavez, is not important. We see the consequences of lack of charisma in the persona of Maduro in Venezuela today. A well intentioned man but to compare him to a giant like Chavez would be unfair.

Even the opposition recognizes Chavez's personality was a huge advantage to him in carrying out his cause for social change, which he called social justice. Chavez united people even more than his hero Simon Bolivar. There are a number of Chavistas, who in-spite of Chavez having been close to Maduro, do not support him, the alternative, the jailed fascist Lopez or neocon Capriles, however, are quite worse and are part of the bourgeois class. Cabello is an alternative from the Chavista camp, but he is still allied with Maduro, and since he lost his place in the Congress is the new VP. Is this a way to distance the Chavez family from politics? Indeed, the son in law of Chavez was the VP, who has even less charisma than Maduro himself. The opposition of Lopez-Capriles, ironically both are related to

Bolivar, and are distant cousins. But rather than get into the details of internal politics of another nation let us move on.

The biggest obstacle to progress is disorganization. Coupled with cowardice or lack of leadership even the best intentions will come to nothing. The perfect example is Alexis Tsipras, leader of the remnants of the Syriza party currently ruling Greece. Since my last book Tsipras himself has turned into a pariah in many left circles, and rightly so. He gave into pressure. Is he a traitor? No. Is he a political coward who lacks leadership? Yes. Let us hope the situation with Podemos in the current election in Spain is not the same. Pablo Iglesias much show leadership. There is such a thing as organized Anarchism, and it is also Socialistic, although to a lot of people this is a contradiction, like Anarcho Capitalism, which I am against. But like I said in my last book not all contradictions are bad. During the Spanish Civil War for a time the Socialists and Anarchists united in-spite of differences and forms their own ideology so there is a history there that is good and could reoccur. A dangerous personality that threatens the so-called minorities of the US is that of Donald Trump, my next chapter will deal with the Trump complex.

Chapter II

The Trump Complex, How Activists Can Fight It

Image of the infamous presidential candidate Trump, grandson of a draft dodger deported from Germany, son of a KKK member, and draft dodger himself. He wants to deport "criminal immigrants" his grandfather was one himself, among his grandfather's criminal professions was pimping and coning people in Real Estate. This is the origins of his riches he is anything but "self-made" he is part of the myth of US Capitalism. I met him in person about 10 years ago in Miami, back when he was a Dem.

He is much like Francisco Franco, Mussolini and Hitler in his traits. Am now going to share a recent article I wrote on this character of Trump, who has turned into an infamous figure in many circles, even among conservatives. I wrote an article questioning if he was the new Hitler (who many forget was elected to power), but this article is one I wrote after that. It has been posted on my blog with word press here is the link:

https://alrsuarez.wordpress.com/2015/12/12/unpublished-article-on-trum

The Editor In Chief of Citizen Roots Magazine, initially did not want my article on Trump, my "friend" Bobby Cuomo was able to convince him otherwise after a few months, but then the Editor responded with graphic criticism against me for the article am about to post. I responded by asking if he would accept a revised version, after a couple weeks I still got no response from him or Bobby, Bobby apparently does not check his voicemail. I have given up trying to get it published with them, I have other people I can publish it with and am now going to do so with a blog. Facebook notes does not let you tag people anymore, so I will rely on a blog for a big portion of my writing. For those who don't know me I am Al R Suarez, investigative journalist, activist and writer out of Tampa, Fl. By the way, since this article was written Trump has said something even more crazy about Muslims which has garnered a lot of anger towards him and even some financial loss like when he spoke against Mexicans, that no Muslims should be allowed to enter the US.

Sidenote since this was posted I was able to clear things up with Bobby.

The Two Americas

By Al R Suarez

At the insistence of my friend Mr. Cuomo, am writing an article on Trump, but it is much more than that. It is not an article written with hate, nor is it written since I feel indebted to him for the spectacular interview he did with me for this magazine. At the risk of sounding arrogant, let me state sincerely. I am writing this article because I feel America needs it. I am writing this article because I feel humanity needs it. Therefore, I will give it my best effort. Journalism, as is activism, is a service to the public. We are giving back to the community, activists who have not found a profession and get welfare one way or another are criticized, but is the activism they do not a service to inform and inspire the public to make the country better? What is journalism? Was what Greenwald did working with Snowden journalism? Why do people like Trump consider Snowden a traitor? We will get into that. I digress. My original article on Trump was entitled: "Is Trump The New Hitler?". This was published in the People's Tribune, a paper I respect out of Chicago, and was translated to Spanish specifically for the immigrant/refugee community.

None of my friends or family support Trump that I know of, but I have some acquaintances who do, particularly classmates, but I have hope they can change their minds. Some people told me they did not like the comparison, even though they despised Trump. Some of these people's opinion I respect so let me clarify. I was not comparing him to Hitler, I was asking a question. A question even a Republican rival of Trump Mr. Kasich had made. Since my original article was written some months ago, Trump has come out with more and more statements that people who know history, especially Germany history leading up to WWII are feeling alarmed over, hence Kasich's question on Trump, which Trump has threatened to suite over, but Trump is a public figure and is therefore fair game. In fact the media in my opinion has been too soft on him. Since I started my new podcast on blogtalkradio with classmate Andrea, we have continued to call out this media as the "Lamestream media".

Trump has recently called for Muslims to wear patches to identify themselves, and has called to close Mosques. If we imagine the Star of David, and synagogue, you replace the words it is almost Hitler verbatim. Recently, even the Anti-Defamation League (ADL), an organization that dedicates itself to fighting anti-Semitism, has even come out against Trump. Being part Jewish, and seeing how the ADL has gone after Islamophobes, even prior to Trump, I respect much of what they do. Trump made fun of a disabled journalist imitating his condition since the reporter backed off on his false claims Muslims were celebrating in New Jersey on 911. Trump claims he didn't know he was disabled, but evidence has come out him and Trump were old friends so he knew this well. But some of his supporters thinks this is coincidental, that Trump forgot they were friends? Such is the logic, or lack their of, of fanaticism. Beating up BLM protesters, and homeless Hispanics, is fine according to Trump, as these acts, and censoring of the press coverage of his events, continue. When this happened, Trump making fun of the disabled, I asked my mother, is Trump going to round up the disabled too?

Anyone who knows history knows what Hitler did with the disabled. The bad of history is bound to repeat itself when we forget. Trump's lies get worse and worse, and yet his supporters say he is the most honest of the candidates. Being blunt and being honest are two different things. Getting caught in lies by so-called reporters who usually cozy up to politicians, especially their fellow "conservatives" on Fox News, means you have to be a pretty bad liar. I like to give the analogy, the man is preparing for heart surgery, and they ask him who he wants to conduct the surgery, he says, someone who is not a doctor. That is the equivalent of wanting the commander & chief to not be a politician. Which is to say politicians are corruptible, but you want someone who knows about politics to be the one who conducts it in the heart of the nation. Carson is no better. The Black Trump has called for a larger wall on the Mexican border, at least he acknowledges one is there already, it's as if they are competing over who can be the most racist. Russophobia, Islamophobia, anti-Hispanic free for all. Carson is actually in the Mideast right now, I am surprised he has not been deported, when he has made statements like a Muslim president could not be president of the US. But at least he is not calling Obama a Muslim right? That is as false as calling Obama a Socialist. Mind you I do not call Carson Dr. Carson, or call Trump Mr. Trump, they do not deserve that respect.

When I say the Two Americas, am not talking about immigrant or non-immigrant. That would be a huge margin difference, especially if we took descendants of immigrant, since the Native American or First Nations people of this continent only comprise about 1% of the population. Am talking about two forces, one I feel is stronger than the other. I am talking about those that represent love and empathy, and those that represent hate and fear. Love is stronger. When I talk about Trump it is personal. In my former public speaking class where I talked about Immigration VS Refugees, and how refugees under international law are granted protections immigrants are not, I was given an F for this speech. Am both pro immigrant and pro refugee mind you, my father is an immigrant. The professor of the public speaking class, had made prior pro Trump and anti-refugee statements, this was beyond playing devil's advocate. The speech was impeccable and heavily cited, and my former philosophy professor is looking at it to give a second opinion. But until now the Dean (am not claiming the Dean or his assistant are racist or self-haters, they are black and Hispanic, but are certainly anti-student on many of their stances) has resisted reconsidering the grade, and I do not have time to make an appeal. While this is going on my mother, an academic herself, has expressed her will to take in Syrian refugees. This makes me proud. That her and so many in America, even after the Paris attacks, which I plan to write about in a future article, can out of love and solidarity make this offer. Bush Jr coined the phrase "compassionate conservatism" does this have to be a contradiction? I talk about contradictions in our society in my latest book which is being translated to Spanish. Can there be a left-right alliance in the US that can be effective? Can Bernie be effective? Even

Bernie in the first democratic debate says there needs to be a penalty against Snowden for "breaking the law". A European conservative like Chirac, who as leader of France was the only one to step up to Bush in 03', is certainly to the left of most American Democrats.

Dr. Jill Stein of the Green Party is the only candidate who said Snowden has paid his dues and should return a hero. Snowden gave up his life of luxury in Hawaii in 2013, and ended up in exile. To me he is a true patriot who revealed how the government spies on us and oppresses our rights. Our nation needs to be one of love, not considering our own people or allies the enemy. If we truly want to fight terror we should fight the terror among ourselves first, like domestic terrorists, who is called by the lamestream the "gunman", who committed the massacre at Planned Parenthood, in part because of false claims by the GOP, who clearly are inciting violent acts. Words matter. One person is called a thug, another a terrorist, why? Because of their race? Should they not be judged on their acts? What Snowden did was an act of heroism or treason? Are the people really the enemy? My hope is the America of true progress can prevail, so future generations do not have to give in to violence or fear, but see more of the similarities than differences in one another at home and abroad. Journalism is a tool that can be used to educate, to spread love, and also to propagandize and spread hate. In this sense the options are simple. The truth hurts, but ultimately can be used for good. Hitler said conscience is a Jewish invention. I believe in the conscienceless of all humanity. We must learn from the lessons of the past, and as a young nation, mature. Having lived abroad, being back in college at a crossroad in my life, I feel now is the time more than ever to write and be heard, so that my nation can avert a catastrophe, which would be electing Trump who we cannot underestimate as Hitler was. I am not trying to make fear. But state the truth as I see it. No matter the hateful forces the people can see through this, as they are in Paris, as they are even when violent acts happen, the beauty of humanity can still prevail, true humanity, that is the side of America of my dreams, that is the side of America I want for my children...

In Solidarity,

Al R Suarez

Host of Vanguard Youth Radio

Trump is someone who if he came to power there could be civil war. That may be a good thing in the long run however. I mentioned earlier the "spectacular interview" with Mr. Bobby Cuomo, AKA Robert Anthony Cuomo, am going to post it here, it gives you a reflection into my inner thinking as an activist, and you can better understand me as an author and reporter of truth this way. Link: http://www.citizenrootsmagazine.com/activism-and-more.html

Image of reporter and activist Bobby Cuomo

Activism and More

In 2015 there are more outlets for political thirst than ever before. So, where do you get your political news and commentary from? Whether you choose your own Twitter, Facebook or Reddit feed to be your morning newspaper, or the ever growing amount of online news publications (like this one), one thing is certain: Radio, Newspaper and TV news are losing chunks of their audience every single year. Mostly, because of their sensationalistic approach to covering serious subject matter and well, their audience is literally dying. The average age viewer of CNN and MSNBC is 60 years old. The average age viewer of Fox News is a paltry 68 years old.

What has been branded the "lamestream" media, (CNN, Fox News, ABC, CBS and MSNBC) has been the defacto fourth branch of the government for some time. They constantly miss the bus on vital stories, misrepresent grassroots movements and politicize everything. And on top of all of that, Brian Williams is a liar, Bill O' Reilly is a hack, Don Lemon is telling black activists to be less loud, Wolf Blitzer and Richard Quest are still trying to find the Malaysia Flight 370 in the Indian Ocean, Al Sharpton can't decide if he wants to report the news or exploit it, and the above mentioned "journalists" all work for one of only six companies who own 90 percent of all American media.

And to make matters worse, the odds of getting any sense making intellectual with logic and reason to report truth and to commentate with dignity takes years of moving up the ass kissing ladder. And by the time you get there, you're like Martin Luther King in a 9th grade classroom in some rural high school in Oklahoma: well behaved and neutered.

Mainstream media is depressing. Which is why the rises in independent online media and political podcasts are about as refreshing as an old episode of the Daily Show with Jon Stewart. Which really sucks, because now that he's gone where is that fat chunk (17 percent) of 18-29 year olds going to get their dependable news from? I think that that answer is independent media, with podcasts leading the revolution.

Podcasts have been a rather new face in the world of media the last decade and have been giving voice and strength to the everyday American. Non-mainstream journalists, activists and commentators all have the opportunity to get their message and truth out to the entire world and many of these podcasts become successes and have large audiences.

Al Suarez is the former host of the successful podcast, Voice of Rebellion Radio and now hosts Peruvian Rebel Radio along side co-host Luciano de la Vega. Suarez is an extremely present political activist and author who believes that podcasts are a tool not only for the future but are changing the way the political process works right now. He has been active in the podcast scene for 6 years.

Suarez is known for his foreign policy commentary on the crisis in Syria, Ukraine and Palestine. Being an activist heavily involved in Occupy Boston, he now resides in Tampa Bay where he airs his current podcast and works with grassroots activism. His most recent podcast covered the Donald Trump fiasco. I got a chance to sit and chat with Suarez about his podcast, activism as a whole, and the political climate in the United States.

Robert Anthony Cuomo: I remember first hearing Al Suarez on a podcast I came across about in 2012 after the Occupy movement had kind of leveled off. And here was this guy with red beret with this East Coast swagger speaking of revolutionary activism and foreign policy. I was intrigued. So, why did you start a podcast? Why was it important for you to do that?

Al Suarez: I am currently hosting along side Luciano de la Vega Peruvian Rebel Radio. We call it that since I am half Peruvian and Luciano is Peruvian American, a comrade out of Philly. Before that I was on various shows stemming back from my return to the States from Europe in 2009, by '10 I was hosting out of blogtalkradio. I was on different networks but most of my radio has been out of there. I did have a radio show at my College. One of the first people I interviewed after I ended my participation in Occupy, back in 2012, was Chomsky. I think he has only been on blogtalkradio with one other host, so people can find the interview. Anyway it has always been my intention to use radio to give an alternative voice, especially for Latin people, as I tried to get Latin people to start Occupy Radio in Boston. I am one of the founders of the old Latin Occupy called Ocupemos El Barrio, which started out of East Boston where my grandparents were from.

RAC: Why are activist podcasts important to the success of movements?

AS: It is hard to know the particular views of a comrade only seeing them in rallies where there is a lot of noise, and often confusion, and pepper spray coming your way. Through podcasts we can find a safe place and do a radio problem, exchanging views and finding commonality, and sharing these views with the masses and others who are part of the campaign or activist workgroup with you.

RAC: How do podcasts differ from the dinosaur outlets of mainstream media?

AS: I consider the mainstream media lamestream. Alternative is authentic. More people use it every day. Corporate media is fake. It is in bed with the government.

RAC: What's your most interesting podcast moment?

AS: My most interesting moment was interviewing Noam Chomsky. He is a hard man to interview. He goes on tangents.

RAC: You have written three books thus far. The first one titled Solidarity Forever? which I have read that dives right into your experiences with the Occupy movement. Your second was The Unfinished Revolution: Post Occupy Analysis. And you just recently published The Vanguard Faction. What can a person who has never heard of Al Suarez expect to learn from your latest book?

AS: It would be hard to understand my latest book without first reading my other two. It is a continuation of them. However, the first book did not deal so much with ideas but with a semi-autobiographical account of my participation in Occupy throughout the East Coast living on camps and going on the frontlines at every opportunity. My new book The Vanguard Faction really emphasizes the role of the youth in activism, and how they can unite factions. This can be applied to many cultures not just the US.

RAC: What are your thoughts on Black Lives Matter? What do you think about their tactics such as Black Brunch (where they interrupt restaurants serving brunch to promote their cause)?

AS: I'm not familiar with Black Brunch. Of course I am aware of BLM as I have marched with them in Tampa and Philly. They are a new movement predominately comprised of youth and so-called minorities. I'm sure a Brown Lives Matter is to follow suit, and like occupy they seem to be unorganized with various offshoot groups and have different groups with different tactics some more what you might call militant, other more non violent. A kind of Malcolm X VS a MLK in tactics. Ideology is not clear either. In principle I support them and am confident they will learn from mistakes and take history into account. They are for human rights rather than just civil, with an emphasis on black lives, with ongoing police brutality, which stats have shown have increased.

RAC: The tactics of policing have increased in brutality for decades. I would argue that not many people, especially the youth know anything about the 1985 Philadelphia bombings constructed by local polices forces.

AS: If you know the facts of the police in the US this is no surprise. With militarization, small towns getting tanks, and the emphasis on hiring veterans, many with PTSD, and trained to deal with an occupied people rather than serve the community at home. There is even news of Mossad(the Central Intelligence Agency of Israel), having trained US police departments, so the blacks could be treated as a Palestinian or an Iraqi rather than a US citizen with equal rights under the law.

This and the hiring practices with an emphasis on cops with a low IQ and being insensitive, as I interviewed former Philly Police Captain Ray Lewis on, you have a deadly combination. Let alone the fact police unions have been corrupted and give racist cops impunity, including cops who discriminate against poor or working class whites. The so-called justice system also is complicit in this, and the various portrayals by the lamestream media, in particular Fox News. The elites always try to divide on race not social class, a poor white man has more in common with a poor black man than a poor white man has in common with, lets say Trump, who pretends to be anti-establishment but is very much a part of it in the charade we know as the US elections.

RAC: What are your thoughts on BLM interrupting leaders to get their message out? Was this a hurtful tactic or helpful?

AS: So what Bernie and others were inconvenienced by a BLM group? There are bigger problems. Bernie is not the solution, however he is certainly far to the left of Hillary, who is not the ideal candidate either. Until we make the essential changes to assure a third party or independent person can get power, we will continue to rely on the unreliable reform, rather than the radical revolutionary change we need. Concern for the middle class is mostly not legitimate, working class needs to be looked at.

RAC: Do you think that Occupy is dead? Or is the legacy the creation of today's current climate of activism? Can Black Lives Matter thank the tactics of Occupy for their current success?

AS: I think BLM can thank more the history of the 60s and 70s, whether the panther Malcolm types, or the MLK types. As you know I wrote a book about Occupy, but I do not want to delve into speculation how dead or alive the movement is at this point, or what my friend Chomsky calls 'the tactic', as they were never really a movement, but planted seeds. Certainly the plant is growing in the form of BLM to a degree. Of course (Occupy) was the direct legacy of the Egyptian and Spanish revolts in particular. Literally Spaniards and Egyptians came to NY in 2011 to train occupiers. They rarely get credit for this.

RAC: You spent much time in Occupy Boston and Occupy Tampa. What was your part in Occupy movement and how has it affected you and the activist community?

AS: I was what you can call a potential leader. Especially to my comrades in Boston before the defamation campaign was planned and implemented against me in full force as described in my first book. As usual, COINTELPRO was in full effect, at least in the major cities where occupy had a presence, and all the potentials that propped up were discredit one way or another. I was arrested twice for the movement, went through much sacrifice and disappointment, and it taught me a valuable lesson on how to trust people in revolutionary politics and the importance of unity. I am now focusing on my activism at college, which has caused me some problems but I have been able to progress and take part in my environmental club. As I told my comrades in Tampa, we must fight from the camps to the campuses, it is time to adapt, which is what real revolutionaries do, and we shall not remain on our armchairs. The time to take it to the streets is coming. Occupy camps are done, but we still have a role in activism. This is an international movement as well. We should not forget that and constrain ourselves to nationalism. We should take the time to study tactics and see how they are effective, what context to use them, etc. Socialism is the only way to acquire the equality we seek. United with different groups but with the same aims is essential.

RAC: The Presidential race is heating up. And there is a list of bozo's who can potentially do some real damage to this country. I know you don't swing with any political party. Who do you support in the presidential election and why?

AS: No one.

RAC: Seriously though? There's no one?

AS: I was thinking of Green Party candidate Jill Stein again, who I met once, but I question some of her domestic policies, such as her stance on gun laws. She seems to be a reformist slightly to the left of Sanders. I am for sane gun laws. Obviously we do not want to see what was passed in Georgia where you can enter a bar with a concealed weapon, and people die from it. Even in the Wild West you checked your gun at the saloon. If former governor Jesse Ventura runs as a Libertarian, I may support him. He is certainly to the left of the Pauls (Ron or Rand). Not quite a Chomsky-type Libertarian, but he is near there. I respect him, and like that he lives part of the year in Mexico. It is smart he has distanced himself from Trump.
 Ventura did good in his one term in his home state, and I am sure as president he could do some good, but again, the system is set against third parties. That would not stop me from voting someone who has the same values as me. I do not even know if Stein will run with Cheri Honkala again. Cheri is a personal friend. If she gets into the race I would probably opt to vote for the Greens after all. By the way I met Trump before when he was a Dem. He is a hypocrite in every way.

RAC: But seriously, if you were held at gunpoint and had to vote for a Republican who would it be? Democrat, who would it be?

AS: If you know anything about me, you know I would not be intimidated by a gun. Several snipers, police and a bulldozer were sent after a few dozen comrades and myself in Boston when they shut the camp down, and I did not budge. Being thrown in the patty wagon and fighting it in court when offered a deal, being one of the few to carry on. When you join the revolution, you understand you are already dead and live your life accordingly, Che Guevara said this well. Trotsky himself reserved himself to the fact Stalin would not let him live, and when he could have left Mexico, he stayed. Malcolm could have moved to Africa, but he faced his fate as well. I'm not comparing myself to anyone, but I would be very lucky if in a few years I did not end up in a jail or killed; either by a fake suicide, which happened to a comrade of mine, or other means. But someday there will be justice for future generations. I try to be optimistic and honor our political prisoners and those who have fallen in the cause.

RAC: Craziest thing you have seen in live person in activism?

AS: NYPD beating a 16 year old girl. At Zucotti Park at Occupy New York in front of cameras and angry people the cops distracted and provoked us. They then opened up the blouse and proceeded to beat a 16 year old girl who is believed to have not even been part of the protest. And then they grabbed and arrested my friend Cecily McMillan and around 70 activists. Including those in a march after Zucotti was attacked where I was almost arrested myself. 50 of us in the end were cornered. About three got out including myself. We stayed in the corner refusing to disperse. People were thrown to the ground, blood was everywhere.

RAC: What are your thoughts on Donald Trump and illegal immigrants?

AS: As I stated earlier, Trump is a hypocrite. He is also dangerous. It is no wonder in my last show I compared him to Hitler. I take my words seriously, as it is not to be funny, Hitler in his campaign in Germany where he ran used similar rhetoric against Jews as Trump has against Mexicans. Hitler was not taken seriously, and we all know the consequences that brought. Journalists need to be tough on Trump and expose him as the phony, and racist, that he is. He cannot get power in this country in politics. A businessman should not be in that role, nor should they be able to bribe as they do. Trump himself had given bribes to Hillary. We need to call things as we see them.

RAC: Any thoughts on Jade Helm?

AS: I have heard of that but I need to look into it more before I comment. Like I said, my words are serious. Before I speculate I need to be well informed on the issue.

RAC: What is the next step for political activism? You call yourself a revolutionary. What does that mean and how do you encourage more ordinary people to come help with this movement?

AS: As Che (Guevara) said, being a revolutionary is the highest of the human species. You do not need to be a Socialist to be a revolutionary, although I consider that ideal. Revolutionaries are leaders in the best sense of the word. They lead by example, and often take the first step when it is time to cross the line and fight for what is right.

The "Rolling Stone" type interview was a success. But the Editor of the magazine obviously was not impressed as he has rejected two articles I submitted on Trump. However, as mentioned in my previous book I was able to get an article published on Trump as well as a Spanish translation, with the People's Tribune, a progressive newspaper out of Chicago which looks out for the poor and "minorities" of the nation. I also got my last book translated to Spanish, it is important to me to reach a Latin audience, from within the US and their own countries or places that have emigrated or took refuge too.

I have written about Central American child refugees, what about Syrian? All these people need to be protected. Anne Frank's family petitioned the US government during the holocaust like countless others, for asylum, were denied, and every member of the family except for the father were killed in a death camp. Most of the world would be considered people of color by the way, hence the quotes with the word minority or as I often put it so-called minority when referring to the darker side of town in the US, as a form of segregation has continued, culminating in the prison system, a slavery for profit system. In a couple generations Anglo Saxons may be the minority in the US, but not if Trump and his cohorts have their way. This is primarily what they fear, they use fear and hate to expand their agenda.

Most recently another BLM protester was attacked at a Trump rally as supporters yelled "Seig Heil" in Nazi fashion, and yelled "burn him!", this is the violence that Trump instigates and supports. Us activists have been called by corporate media "hippies", "lazies", told to get a job. When Bush Jr told Michael Moore to get a real job, he produced Fahreinheit 911, which probably did more than any film to discredit Bush. Do not underestimate an activist and a pen, as they say, the pen is mightier than the sword. Bush is in there with Nixon and Truman as the least popular US presidents in history.

The Trump complex is the poor white guy blaming the black guy with a job routine, how these losers go against their own interest and give up their money to the "tea party" which is nothing like the actual Boston Tea Party who were anti-imperialists during the American Revolution, to put in the pockets of rich snobs born with billions like Trump. There is no converting these chumps to the left, that is the chumps who follow Trump like chipmunks, who want a piece of bread, and will break off their own loaf to get it and say thank you as they starve themselves and give the remaining loaf to their oppressor. Do they not realize they have more in common with a poor or working class black man than a fellow white guy who is rich?

Most people on welfare in the US are Anglo Saxon in red or Republican states, so the whole "blacks on welfare" or "Dem blacks on welfare" routine is false, are there ghettos? Yes. But who started them? As I have stated prior, it was the own government, look at the origins, see who is to gain keeping the poor down. ISIS? How did they start? Western intelligence agencies, follow the paper trail, like a good Capitalist, ya?

I digress. That is my one and only attempt trying to get through the madness of the Trump crowd in this book besides the article. A poor attempt I admit, but I think my article in retrospect came off as a bit soft so I am reiterating my disgust, especially with recent events, with the Trump scum. Bullies that they are. We need to fight back. And yes Hispanics and Muslims need to arm themselves and defend their barrios or communities from the onslaught of the Trump barbarians. Am talking organized militias not gangs or vigilantes. There is a bit of humor in this to maintain sanity, but deep down am quite serious and not being sarcastic. Of course we must maintain the moral high-ground. Not lower to their level.

Conclusion

Let me conclude by talking about revolutionary sacrifice, this sacrifice means giving it your all in-spite of whether you will win or lose, and not going down without a fight. Never expect gratitude. No good deed goes unpunished. But remember this is for the future. Future generations. We need more than education, we need to fight back. We need a spiritual revolution of consciousness, then a physical revolution can come about…

Image of author

www.ingramcontent.com/pod-product-compliance
Lightning Source LLC
Chambersburg PA
CBHW040318010626
45792CB00023B/1018